# Contents

# Shops and markets

If you want to buy something, you usually go to a shop or a market.

Some shops sell just one or two types of thing. This shop in Ethiopia sells pans. Other shops sell a wide range of goods. You might find clothes, pots and pans, and food all on sale in one shop.

## Titles in this series:
Clothes Around the World
Festivals Around the World
Food Around the World
Houses Around the World
Musical Instruments Around the World
Shops and Markets Around the World
Toys and Games Around the World
Transport Around the World

**Cover pictures:** (Clockwise from top) A floating market in Thailand. A Sikh trader selling cloth in Calcutta, India. Market traders in Solola, Guatemala. Choosing apples in a supermarket, UK.

**Contents page:** A bakery in Paris, France.

Book editor: Alison Cooper
Series editor: Deb Elliott
Book design: Malcolm Walker
Cover design: Simon Balley

First published in 1995 by Wayland Publishers Ltd,
61 Western Road, Hove, East Sussex BN3 1JD

This edition published in 1999 by Wayland Publishers Ltd

© Copyright 1995 Wayland Publishers Ltd

Find Wayland on the Internet at http://www.wayland.co.uk

**British Library Cataloguing in Publication Data**
Hall, Godfrey
    Shops and Markets Around the World –
    (Around the World Series)
    I. Title II. Series
    381.1

ISBN 0 7502 2567 X

Typeset by Kudos Design Services
Printed and bound in Italy by G. Canale & C.S.p.A.

Thanks to Ulrike and Reinhard Bätz,
and Sue Hall.

**Picture Acknowledgements**
The publishers would like to thank the following for allowing their pictures to be reproduced in this book: J Allan Cash 6, 20, 21, 26; Eye Ubiquitous *cover* (top right, C Johnson), 9 (bottom, Pam Smith), 13 (top, C Johnson; bottom, David Cumming), 24, 27 (bottom, Paul Stuart), 29 (top), 29 (bottom, David Cumming); Godfrey Hall 7 (top); Robert Harding *cover* (top left), 4, 5, 9 (top, Adam Woolfitt), 18 (Gavin Hellier), 25, 28; Panos Pictures 7 (bottom, Jim Holmes), 19 (top, Sean Sprague); Peter Sanders 10, 19 (bottom), 27 (top); Tony Stone Worldwide *cover* (bottom left, Don and Pat Valenti; bottom right), *contents page* and 8 (Steven Rothfeld), 11 (Don and Pat Valenti), 14 (Suzanne and Nick Geary), 15 (top, Rex A Butcher; bottom, Ed Pritchard), 16 (John Freeman), 17, 22 (Rohan), 23 (Lorne Resnick); Wayland Picture Library (APM Studios) 12. Commissioned photographs arranged by Zoë Hargreaves.

# shops and markets
## around the world

## Godfrey Hall

**WAYLAND**

Markets started when people got together to exchange fruit and vegetables they had grown, or things they had made. You can find markets in cities, towns and villages all around the world. Many people travel a long way to sell their goods in the market.

# The village shop

The village shop is an important part of village life. People can meet there for a chat and buy everyday goods, such as milk or newspapers. Going to the village shop saves them having to travel to the nearest town.

This village shop in the eastern part of Germany is crammed with goods. There is hardly room for the shopkeeper.

Mobile shops are used in many countries. The goods are usually carried in a car or van, although this mobile-shop owner is carrying his goods in baskets. Mobile shops visit several villages each day.

# The bakery

Bread and cakes are sold at a bakery. The bread in this shop comes in all different shapes and sizes.

In some countries, people visit the bakery each morning to buy their bread. The baker has to get up very early to bake the bread, ready for the first customers.

In hot countries, such as India, bakers often work outside making the bread.

# Supermarkets

Large supermarkets sell many different things, from fruit and vegetables to kitchen equipment and clothes. Some even have their own chemist who can sell medicines.

Supermarkets are found all over the world. This one is in Riyadh, in Saudi Arabia.

In a supermarket, you pick the goods you want
to buy from the shelves and put them in your
basket or trolley. You pay for your shopping at
the check-out.

# Buying clothes

Some shops, like this one, sell lots of different sorts of clothes – shirts, trousers, dresses, skirts, socks and shoes. Other shops sell just one type of clothes.

In some parts of the world, people make their own clothes. They buy material from a shop or market stall.

Sometimes, clothes are made by a tailor. This is a village tailor hard at work in India.

# Shopping arcades

Shopping arcades and malls are very popular. There are lots of shops inside one big building. Shopping malls are often built on the edge of towns, and people enjoy visiting them for a day out.

The shops in an arcade or mall are usually built on several floors, which are connected by escalators and lifts. Some malls also have places where people can eat if they get tired and hungry.

Building lots of shops together under one roof is not a new idea. This is the Burlington Arcade in London, Britain. It was built in 1819 – nearly two hundred years ago.

# Department stores

Shops that are very big, with many different things sold in separate parts of the shop, are called department stores. This famous department store is called GUM. It is in Moscow in Russia.

Many department stores are in beautiful old buildings. The Galeries Lafayette store in Paris, France, has a lovely glass ceiling.

# Outdoor markets

Markets are held in open spaces, such as the town square, and the traders often display their goods on stalls. Brightly coloured canopies protect the goods from the rain or sun.

Markets can be very big and busy, and people sometimes travel a long way to buy and sell their goods. The market is also a good place to meet your friends.

This is a livestock market in Morocco, where farmers have come to buy and sell sheep and other animals.

# Indoor markets

Markets can be held indoors as well as outside. Many British towns have market halls, like this one in Lincolnshire. People can enjoy shopping in the market even when the weather is cold and wet.

This is the indoor market in Funchal, Madeira.

# Bazaars

Bazaars are held in Africa and the Middle East. 'Bazaar' is the old Persian name for a market. In the bazaar, the traders and shoppers are usually protected from the hot sun by a roof or canopy.

Bazaars can be very exciting places to visit. They are usually crowded with people buying and selling. The smell of spices and other foods drifts from stall to stall.

# Fish markets

Fish markets are often held early in the morning, when the fishermen return from a night at sea in their boats. The boats are unloaded and the fish are sold at the quayside. Local people hurry to the harbour to see what they can buy.

In some cities, such as Bangkok in Thailand, they have floating markets. Fish and many other types of food are piled up in boats and sold along the river.

# Market traders

People who work in a market usually have to get up early. When they arrive at the market, they might have to set up their stalls and put out what they are going to sell. The traders call to people passing by, to tempt them to buy their goods.

This market trader is weighing some nuts for a customer.

This is a camel market in Egypt. The men are choosing the camel they want to buy and haggling over the price.

# Special markets

Some markets are held only at certain times of the year. Christmas markets are popular in Germany. People can buy Christmas decorations, and there are also stalls selling hot wine and food.

In the summer, craft fairs are held in many British villages. Traditional skills such as patchwork and wood-carving are often used to make the goods on sale.

All sorts of old items are sold at antique markets – paintings, jewellery, clocks, china. Some of these are worth a lot of money. People enjoy browsing round the stalls, hoping to pick up a bargain.

# Glossary

**bargain**   Something sold for a low price. People usually say something is a bargain if it is cheaper than they expected it to be.

**browsing**   Looking at goods for sale in an unhurried way.

**canopies**   Coverings, often made of cloth, used as roofs.

**exchange**   To swap, to change something for something else. Long ago people might have exchanged some fruit they had grown for some eggs, instead of paying for the eggs with money.

**goods**   Objects that are for sale.

**haggling**   Arguing over how much to pay for something.

**harbour**   A sheltered place where boats are kept when they are not out at sea.

**patchwork**   Sewing small pieces of material together in a pattern.

**Persian**   From Persia, the old name for the country that is now called Iran.

**quayside**   The place in the harbour where boats are loaded and unloaded.

**spices**   Flavourings made from parts of plants.

**stalls**   Tables where goods are set out for sale in a market.

**traders**   People who sell goods in a market.

**traditional skills**   Ways of working that have been used for a very long time.

# Books to read

*Shopkeeper* (*Working Worldwide* series) by Margaret Hudson (Wayland, 1996)

*Shopping* by Gill Tanner and Tim Wood (A & C Black, 1993)

*Shops and Markets* (*Stepping Through History* series) by Peggy Burns (Wayland, 1995)

30

# More information

**Would you like to find out more about the people and places you have seen in the photographs in this book? If so, read on.**

**pages 4–5**
A pan shop in Harar, Ethiopia.
The market in Djenne, Mali.

**pages 6–7**
The village shop in Grundisburgh, Suffolk, Britain.
The village shop in Eichicht in the eastern part of Germany.
A mobile shop in Bangladesh. Mobile shops are found across the world in areas where the villages are too small to support their own shop.

**pages 8–9**
A bakery in Paris, France.
A French woman leaving a bakery in the Loire region.
Unleavened bread being fried outdoors in the Kashmir region of India.

**pages 10–11**
The first shop where customers served themselves, rather than having goods weighed and measured for them by shop assistants, was opened in 1916 in the USA. From this grew Piggly Wiggly, the first supermarket chain. Supermarkets did not catch on in Britain until the 1950s, when the now-famous chains Waitrose and Sainsbury's opened their first self-service stores.

**pages 12–13**
A Marks & Spencer store in Brighton, Britain. Marks & Spencer has branches in many parts of the world.
A Sikh trader selling cloth in Calcutta, India.
A village tailor in Jaisalmer, India.

**pages 14–15**
The New Queen Victoria Building shopping arcade in Sydney, Australia.
A shopping mall in Dusseldorf, Germany.
Although arcades like the Burlington Arcade had been in existence for many years, large enclosed shopping malls did not develop until after the Second World War. The first enclosed mall opened in Minneapolis, USA, in 1956.

**pages 16–17**
The first department store was Bon Marché, which began in Paris as a small shop in the early nineteenth century. By 1865 it had expanded and been divided into 'departments'.

The first department store chain was begun by J. C. Penney in the USA in the 1920s.
The GUM store, situated in Red Square in Moscow, opened in 1921. It offered consumer goods which were not available in most stores in the Communist bloc, and attracted tourists from all over the Soviet Union and beyond.

**pages 18–19**
A market in the town square at Brno in the Czech Republic.
The weekly market at Solola in Guatemala.

**pages 20–21**
The market hall in Louth, Lincolnshire, in Britain.
The Friday market at the Mercado dos Lavradores (Workers' Market) in Funchal, Madeira.

**pages 22–3**
A crowded bazaar in Marrakesh, Morocco. In small towns the bazaar is usually found in a single narrow street, but in larger towns it spreads through a network of passageways.
A stall holder in Sousse, Tunisia.

**pages 24–5**
Traders selling fish from the boats at Galata Bridge in Istanbul, Turkey.
A boat in the floating market, Bangkok.

**pages 26–7**
The apple market in Maeown, China.
A nut seller in Delhi, India.
Traders at the camel market in Cairo, Egypt.

**pages 28–9**
The Christmas market in Stuttgart, Germany.
A craft fair being set up in Cornwall, Britain. The stall holders are wearing eighteenth-century-style mobcaps and dresses.
An antique stall and shop in Portobello Road, London, in Britain.

# Index